HOW ANIMALS ADAPT TO SURVIVE

KEEPING WARM with FUR and FAT

HANNAH FIELDS

PowerKiDS press.

New York

Published in 2018 by The Rosen Publishing Group, Inc.
29 East 21st Street, New York, NY 10010

First Edition

Editor: Elizabeth Krajnik
Book Design: Reann Nye

Photo Credits: Cover, p. 1 Robert Haasmann/Shutterstock.com; p. 4 tryton2011/Shutterstock.com; p. 5 Michael Smith ITWP/Shutterstock.com; p. 6 cpaulfell/Shutterstock.com; p. 7 Giedriius/Shutterstock.com; p. 8 Montipaiton/Shutterstock.com; p. 9 Doug Lindstrand/Design Pics/Getty Images; p. 10 MZPHOTO.CZ/Shutterstock.com; p. 11 Design Pics Inc/First Light/Getty Images; p. 12 Don Mammoser/Shutterstock.com; p. 13 Richard Seeley/Shutterstock.com; p. 14 worldswildlifewonders/Shutterstock.com; p. 15 Chase Dekker/Shutterstock.com; p. 17 Donald M. Jones/Minden Pictures/Getty Images; p. 18 Josef Pittner/Shutterstock.com; p. 19 Nigel Pavitt/AWL Images/Getty Images; p. 20 Steven Kazlowski/Science Faction/Getty Images; p. 21 Mircea C/Shutterstock.com; p. 22 Ritesh Chaudhary/Shutterstock.com.

Cataloging-in-Publication Data

Names: Fields, Hannah.
Title: Keeping warm with fur and fat / Hannah Fields.
Description: New York : PowerKids Press, 2018. | Series: How animals adapt to survive | Includes index.
Identifiers: ISBN 9781538328415 (pbk.) | ISBN 9781508164326 (library bound) | ISBN 9781538328477 (6 pack)
Subjects: LCSH: Adaptation (Biology)–Juvenile literature. | Fur–Juvenile literature.
Classification: LCC QH546.A73 2018 | DDC 578.4–dc23

Manufactured in China

CPSIA Compliance Information: Batch #BW18PK: For Further Information contact Rosen Publishing, New York, New York at 1-800-237-9932

CONTENTS

ADAPTING for WINTER

Animals adapt, or change, to better survive their **environments**. Adaptations help animals hide or get away from danger. Some adaptations also help animals fight off predators.

WALRUS

Although not covered in hair or fur, whales are mammals. They breathe air, are warm blooded, and give birth to live babies that drink milk. Whales, dolphins, seals, and walruses are **marine** mammals.

Mammals are warm-blooded animals whose babies drink milk and whose bodies are covered with hair or fur. Warm-blooded animals must keep their body around the same temperature at all times. This requires a lot of energy, which comes from food.

Fur and fat help animals living in colder **climates** use less energy to keep their body at the right temperature. If the animal can't find food, its body will burn stored fat to produce energy.

SPECIAL WOOL

Musk oxen are hairy mammals that live in Arctic areas of Canada, Alaska, and Greenland. The hair covering a musk ox's body is thick and grows to be about 2 feet (0.61 m) long, almost touching the ground. Under this hair, the musk ox has a layer of thick, soft wool called qiviut (KEE-vee-uht). Short hair covers the musk ox's face.

The musk ox sheds its wool in summer. During the warmer months, the hairy **herbivores** eat more grasses and plants. The food they eat is stored as fat to keep them warm and give them energy during the winter months.

KEEPING WARM with the MUSK OX

MUSK OX BASICS

Males and females come together for two months in late summer to **mate**. After eight months, female musk oxen give birth to one calf each. Herds of musk oxen circle their young and point their horns toward a predator if they feel **threatened**. The way they gather together makes it easy for humans to hunt them for their meat and supersoft wool.

Adaptation Answers

When they cannot eat grass because it is covered in snow, female musk oxen can use the energy stored in their fat to help produce milk to feed their calves.

After just a few hours, newborn musk ox calves can keep up with their mothers and herds. This helps keep them safe from predators.

Musk ox qiviut is eight times warmer than sheep wool and is softer than **cashmere**. However, qiviut is very rare. This makes it a very valuable fiber for making clothing. Musk oxen almost died out because they were overhunted. Today, laws protect them from being hunted.

GRIZZLY FACTS

Grizzly bears are one of two species, or kinds, of brown bear found in North America. They live in forests and prairies, as well as meadows located below the woods on very tall mountains. They once roamed throughout the western United States, but their **habitats** have been reduced. Most live in Alaska and northern Canada.

Grizzly bears spend most of their time alone. However, large groups of grizzlies gather when salmon swim upstream in the summer months. The fat from salmon helps grizzly bears survive the winter.

Adult grizzly bears can weigh around 700 pounds (317.5 kg) and live to be about 30 years old. Their fur can be anywhere between tan and dark brown.

Grizzly bears are **omnivores**. They commonly eat plants, fruits, berries, and grass. They also eat salmon, small mammals, deer, and even moose.

WINTER SLEEP

Winter can be a hard time for grizzly bears to find food. During summer and fall, they eat as much food as they can find to build up fat.

Grizzly bears dig a den, or hole, into a hillside. As they settle down to sleep inside, their heart rate slows and their body temperature drops. They live off stored fat while they sleep for up to seven months.

Experts say that bears don't actually **hibernate**. They do sleep most of the winter. True hibernators, such as bats, wake up slowly. However, if a bear is disturbed, it wakes up quickly.

Female grizzly bears give birth to cubs, or babies, in winter months. The mothers use energy from stored fat to produce milk for their cubs. They care for the cubs in the den until they are ready to come out in the spring.

WEASELS of the SEA

Sea otters are one of 13 species of otters, which are part of the weasel family. Sea otters live along the northern coasts of the Pacific Ocean. There are two subspecies of sea otters in the United States: the California, or southern, sea otter, and the Alaskan, or northern, sea otter.

Sea otters often drift on the water's surface. They wrap their body in sea plants growing from the ocean floor to keep from floating away.

Sea otters don't have a protective layer of fat. This means that they can't store energy to use when they're cold. Sea otters eat about 25 percent of their own weight each day because they burn energy so quickly. This energy helps keep their bodies warm.

FANTASTIC FUR

Unlike most marine mammals, which have a thick layer of fat to keep them warm, sea otters depend on their fur to keep warm. Their fur is very thick. They have up to a million hairs per square inch (6,451,600 per sq cm). Most humans only have 100,000 hairs on their heads.

A layer of air gets trapped between sea otters' thick fur and their skin. This protects them from the cold water. It also helps them float. Sea otters spend up to two or three hours a day **grooming** their fur. Dirty or tangled fur will not keep the cold water out.

Adaptation Answers

Sea otters use their paws to clean their fur and fluff it up with air bubbles. They are very **flexible** creatures, so cleaning hard-to-reach places is easy.

Sea otters give birth in the water. They are the only otter species to do this. Mothers hold their babies on their chest while floating on their back.

ARCTIC SURVIVORS

Arctic foxes can be found in the coldest parts of the world, including Alaska, Canada, Greenland, Russia, Norway, Scandinavia, and Iceland. They are 9 to 12 inches (22.8 to 30.5 cm) tall at the shoulder—about the size of a house cat.

Adaptation Answers

Arctic foxes stay active year round, including winter. This is possible because they have a thick layer of fat underneath their fur that keeps them warm in the low Arctic temperatures.

Their small bodies help keep them warm, but their most important feature is their fur. Arctic foxes have thick, multilayered fur that helps them survive temperatures as low as -90° Fahrenheit (-67.7° Celsius). They also have thick fur on their paws that allows them to easily walk across snow and ice.

Arctic foxes mainly eat lemmings, a type of rodent. If they can't find a source of food to hunt, they might eat food left behind by other predators, such as polar bears.

ADAPTING FUR for HUNTING

The Arctic fox has adapted so its fur changes with the seasons. In summer, their coat is brown or gray. This helps them blend in with their summer environment. During the winter, Arctic foxes have a coat of thick, white fur. Not only does the fur keep them warm, it lets them blend in with the ice and snow that are everywhere in winter.

Adaptation Answers

Arctic foxes have special hunting skills. When they hear their prey under the snow, they leap into the air and pounce through the snow on their next meal.

Arctic foxes use their furry tail to shield themselves from the cold wind. This also helps keep their body from losing heat.

By blending in with their surroundings, Arctic foxes have an easier time hunting. The color of their fur makes it easier for them to sneak up on their prey, because the prey can't see them coming.

IS BLUBBER FAT?

Many marine mammals, such as whales and seals, have a thick layer of blubber. This protective layer isn't like the fat that land animals and humans have. It is much thicker than the fat a grizzly bear or musk ox has.

In fact, some scientists don't think of blubber as fat at all. They think of it as a type of connective tissue, or a part of the body that holds together other parts of the body. Blubber connects an animal's internal organs to its skin.

Blubber stores energy and keeps marine mammals warm. It even helps them float!

GLOSSARY

cashmere: The fine wool from the undercoat of the cashmere goat and the yarn made from this wool.

climate: The average weather conditions of a place over a period of years.

environment: The conditions that surround a living thing and affect the way it lives.

flexible: Capable of bending or being bent.

groom: To make someone or something neat and clean.

habitat: The natural home for plants, animals, and other living things.

herbivore: An animal that only eats plants.

hibernate: To spend the winter in an inactive state in which the body temperature drops and breathing slows.

marine: Of or relating to the sea.

mate: To come together to make babies.

omnivore: An animal that feeds on both plants and other animals.

threaten: To show an intention to do harm or something unwanted.

INDEX

WEBSITES

Due to the changing nature of Internet links, PowerKids Press has developed an online list of websites related to the subject of this book. This site is updated regularly. Please use this link to access the list: www.powerkidslinks.com/haas/fur